Arthur Phantomhive

MANIAC

© 2021, Arthur Phantomhive
Printed and published by: BoD - Books on
Demand, Norderstedt
ISBN: 9783755755180

For my CARING FATHER,

I can't forget you.

CONTENT

Mental meltdown

16   BRAINIAC

18   ParadoX?

20   ?

20   ?0

21   CompleX God CompleX – so difficult

24   Lunatic Brainstorming

25   Prisonbreak

26   Lyric Straitjacket

32   Alien Invasion

33   Scientific Enlightment

35   Flashback

CONTENT

Spiritual meltdown

40   Transcending Heavens

42   Tower of Gods and Emperors

44   Demigod

46   Springs Spark

48   A String to Careless

50   ??

51   Deep-Sea-Dystopia

52   Lucifer

CONTENT

Emotional meltdown

58   Choices creations

60   Winter's Sunflowers

62   Our Rebirth

65   ?00

66   Falcons and Butterflies

68   Antisocial

70   Playful

73   Porcelain funeral

CONTENT

Fictional meltdown

77   Murderous clown

79   Bungee-gum

81   Texture Surprise

83   Player's Paradise

85   Berserk

87   King of the Damned

89   Come join me

CONTENT

Trivial meltdown

94   What they say

96   What I say

98   No Brainer

99   ?0?

99   ??0

100   X-Massacre

101   Sturdy Business

104   ???

The Ancient of Days

- William Blake -

Mental meltdown

BRAINIAC

original misunderstood

delusional?

loner rejection

daydreams,

genius

hunger for life, suffering

profound, astute

hunger for love

otherworldly, confused, **brilliant!**

haughty, overlooked, suppressed

madman

brain

MANIAC

Even you love him from afar,

Hate him up close

ParadoX?

In the knots of my mind, I saw the

paradoXes

I observed - engaged and confused

ParadoX - thing of *underconsumption.*

'ParadoX!' I howled,

'Weird, beautiful paradoX!'

Deep into that conflicting darkness

ParadoX – tormentor of my dreams!

I awoke and praised the irrationality

I heard a corollary, misunderstood

contradiction

Narrowly beware

A deep laced thought unravels

out of emptiness

Occult account book

A religious symbol draft

goes hazy in chaos

CompleX God CompleX
–
so difficult

When being is not easy, but difficult

When being GOD is not simple,

but compleX

But if you make it anyway,

Then you are definitely a nice FLEX

You dare to assume a god compleX to

me?

That I really shine is reflected in

everything

Not least in people's belief,

Belief in me

A faith as firmly as in God,

Even my greatest adversaries

Cannot resist my charisma

Of course, a god is also humble

I don't like the self-portrayal,

REALLY

But the ignorance of the masses forces

me

To intervene, to remember, to warn,

Nobody should doubt me

God compleX?

NO - nice FLEX

Who does not recognize yet

-

you will recognize

You will become my admirer

Who does not understand yet

-

you will understand

You will become my student

Who does not believe yet

-

you will believe

You will become my disciple

Three steps to *enlightenment*

Arthur Phantomhive

So deep

So humble

Lunatic Brainstorming

By the Maniac, I saw the ghosts

My loony, I could not awaken

{: The doctrinaire smiled :{

I crave the ideological, individualist

interventionist

I crave the psycho, paranoid prostitute

Take the *obscurantist* from out my heart

Take the crazy from out my heart

Waka – Waka!

Wacko – Wacko!

Prisonbreak

Descending into the eclipse

I await a slaughterman

All my soul within me cracking

Shy gazes, sinister self

With all passion in me fading

There is no tomorrow, no evading

My *childlike tears* reflecting on retribution

Tomorrow - day of eXecution

Lyric Straitjacket

They didn't believe me

They didn't believe in me

Heartlessly they dragged me out of my

ivory tower

They pressed me into a

straitjacket

and drove me away

Body and mind are one in me,

yet conflicted

This is how my sacred ideas became

constricted

They tried everything on me:

Observation

Conversation

Therapy

Medication

Antimasturbation corsets

CoX's swing

Electric shocks

Solitary confinement

Exorcism

...

...

Bloodletting

Lobotomy

Trepanation

They *changed* me

ONLY superficially

Pfffhhh... phpfff...

fishy – fishy

squishy - squishy

They opened my mind

Not only my head

Skullcap breakthrough

TELEPATHY

Multidimensional alien conversation

UNLOCKED

New voices emerged in my head

Like little birds

Yet UFOs to me

Until I listened closely

And they assured my superiority

What a pity

The doctors not even recognized my
premonitions

Still rejected my conditions

So I summoned them to the city

Alien invasion

Portals opening

„Greetings"

Fooling around with my eXtraterrestrial

friends

Beams, screams

everywhere

Rocketbeans, dreams

Acts of terrorism

Freeing *me* from psychiatric prison

Scientific Enlightenment

They didn't believe me

They didn't believe in me

They didn't believe in them

But now that they came

It's such a shame

We must open their minds

Their skulls are already open

Ready to receive the holy X-rays

Recognition *beyond* all sciences

Space-time divides like their minds

psychosis

enlightenment is near

Now they recognize

Now they understand

Now they believe

Flashback

By the grave I saw the end

That moony episode – everlasting

Back into my memories

My nightmare – eternal...

Wha... Whaawhu...hu...

WAAAAAAAH!!!

Back into my mind

My life – finito

Back into *my soul*

And the fears – never distracting

Take this time from out my heart

Death shall bring salvation

Jerusalem Plate 76

- William Blake -

Spiritual meltdown

Transcending Heavens

Much I marvel the outside realm

I desire the saturnian, spaceward

spheres

All my soul within me seeking

Transmuhh, Transsss...

The transmundane terra

incognita

................atmosphere separates..................

me

miii

I discovered the heights

Only this and an obscurity

There is and will be untouchable purity

Tower of gods and emperors never

subjecting

Tower of Gods and Emperors

Shrouded in clouds rises the tower,

High up thrives the seat of power

Where lofty gods reside

And a graceful goddess

Once alive, splendid kings and queens,

Still their glory greens,

Here up in the tower,

Beyond their once limited hopes and
dreams,

Evergreen bloom, their lasting final hour

More than they wanted,

Though they always wanted more,

United lonely at the top,

Locked up and haunted,

In the ulterior golden tower,

Forevermore.

Demigod

Demigod

Storm, Lightning

Powerlust, Control, Fight

Making the world go around

Thunder Gods son

An incomplete god

Needs to be bold.

Half-blood god

Leader of the brave warriors,

The imperfect, the suffering

Thunder Gods son

Loud, Unshakable

Quakes, Clouds, Forces

Never surrender,

DemiGod!

Springs Spark

My passion is a splendid mess

Untidy fountain

A further, confusion blooms

Watching the chaos

Distressful leaping

A last creative spark blooms

Above the old flower

Before it breaks into something new.

PerpleXing leaping

Where eXpression occupies

Watching the whole wood

More haunting than the forgotten old

flower.

A String to Careless

Pale memory

Yesterday is lost

By the broken strings

A line I shouldn't have crossed

Look at the innocently forgotten.

Look at the accidental omission

Look, you are so rotten

Valued, forgotten, again and again

Suspicious claws

Above the old feather

Until the last memory falls

Valued, forgotten, again and again

Light breaks the photos glass

A clear idea

Full of venal brilliance

How predictable and bitter

Overvalued and forgotten again

Vacate outer space

an unholy light burst floods

into the silence

Deep-Sea-Dystopia

Mystical, a shimmering jellyfish

An urban, underworld sinks deeper

Atlantis crushed, inflamed, squished

Sunken home of the dreaded reaper,

The bittersweetness of a collapsing

empire

A burning city, covered in seafire

Lucifer

I suspect a fallen angel to steal my

twisted black heart

I hear the sound of the underworld

begging my domination

I want hell to break,

Heaven to break,

Demons to surrender,

Like I will, angel

I pretend here in hell until then,

My longed-for angel

I feel it coming

I touch your silky skin with my bloody

hand, almost

I worry, hell won't rise,

Heaven won't fall

I understand hell chains never break,

I need an angel to escape

I say nothing at all

I dream silently,

Silently I fall

The Lament for Icarus

- Herbert James Draper -

Emotional meltdown

Choice's creations

Faded break of day

A lovely, lost girl stares

Into the nothingness

Eyes empty, skin fair

Shining aurora

A nice, lovely girl stares

At the warming luminary

Twinkling eyes, skin fair

Bleached break of the day

An older, harsh woman stares

A depth of ages

Her heart heavy, icy hair

Sunshiny morning

An old, fallen woman stares

A love surrenders

Full heart, grey hair

Winter's Sunflowers

My icy frost, you urge me to write.

Your cunning ways to cover and sneak,

Invading my mind

through the starlit nights,

Highest buildings and trees,

Covered till peak

White godforsaken

A little, fluid snowflake

Like winter's sunflower,

Cold beauty awakens

Tender silver charmer,

My favorite seasons armor

Spring takes you, scares my pricey heart,

I'll yearn your magic whilst we're apart.

Trip to the stars

Our Rebirth

For dark temptation, my love

Hate, in a day

A memory of a foggy body

Entangle, in a minute

And I promise we will be

Bound together, I forgive you

Your raven hair, a love through history

We melt into one passion

I gaze upon your silver raven hair, for

we are

Connected together, I share with you

I give you my body

My soul, my dark temptation

A virtue

A starlight, a flower, your passion

tick - tock

a flash - a pulse

In a golden day, I melt into your heart

And I swear we will be

Bound together, I bequeath to you

Your raven hair, a soul through the

universe

We melt into one kiss.

Wicked reservoir

A black clouded shadow strives

beyond the wedding

Falcons and Butterflies

You get on with life as a hunter,

You're a reckless kind of soul

You crave natures mess

You crave to contemplate the sky

But when you start to daydream,

Your mind turns straight to ocean

Sometimes I look into your hunting eyes,

I notice the way you think about flying

with a smile,

Curved lips you just can't disguise

But you think it's depth making your life

worthwhile

Why is it so hard for you to decide

which you love more?

Sky or...

Ocean?

You only use to hang out with falcons

and butterflies,

My friend

Antisocial

Take a bow

I'll hold your hand untiringly, you said

Life burns the soul

Clown of darkness

But I don't want to live

Without your tricks

Repeated, severe

High level of frustration

Getting into fights

May the everlasting fire come upon us

SCARED?

You once promised me an eternity

Bad idea

A moment, B second

Rest in peace

Playful

HA HA HA here comes the J O K E R

Finds his niches

Carries out his knacks

Plays his prey

Until it cracks

A hA HAAa …

Alien eyes

Turns the knife in the wound

Rummages in guts

Disguised as a friend,

Attracts you irresistibly,

Pulls out his knife,

His mesmerizing, versatile knife

His strong, protective knife?

You walk straight into it,

Throw up blood and all your childish

illusions

Betrayed glance of yours

HA HA HA HA HA HAAAA ...

Your silence

JOKER

Porcelain funeral

A pearlwhite goth cries

Over the broken doll

Her voodoo demanded this price

Mirror, mirror on the wall -

Wasn't she beautiful when she crawled?

Near death Dolly fought her tragic faith,

So, her legs needed to break.

Hands and arms, her neck then too,

A banal routine for voodoo.

But Dolly, goth really loved her deeply,

She needs to see her cutely sleeping,

Down her grave, her favorite doll,

But goth would sacrifice them all,

If even just her howling wrath dissolves.

The hatred

- Pietro Pajetta -

Fictional meltdown

Murderous CLOWN

Sadistic = LOVELY

Choatic & MONSTROUS

Peel, shred, LAUGH

I'm a FUNNY mess

Tape up, thrash, ENTERTAIN

Such feelings of PLEASURE

Never ending...

Disturbing CARING FATHER

Bungee-gum

The way you glue, stretch and twist,

Gummy, yummy, tricky substance,

Enemies break, when they get kissed,

By your devilish charm,

I choose you, bungee-gum

I'll use you, bungee-gum

Your sticky feints fill my days

I'll use you in many ways,

Nasty trick, tricky gum

Stretching you, how it tempts me,

Trapping them

My wit will bring a lot of fun,

So, I stick to you, bungee-gum.

TeXture Surprise

Concealing the truth in my favor

Undermining the reasoning of

my prey

You manipulate and deceive wherever

you are

Materialization of my will,

my treachery

I don't only use you for magic tricks

But also in prophecy and poetry

EXpression of my obscure genius

Oh TeXture Surprise,

you are so good

You make me hot, like you should

To reveal the truth of this scripture

You have to sharpen your eyes...

...for teXture surprise

Player's Paradise

There are people, there are players

And a fragmented world within,

The players world of dirty sins

A hidden, tricky place,

A breath of danger is in the air,

Such coldness, no one even cares,

Between wild branches and blurred

shapes,

A violent clash, a deadly game

Risky dice

Where bad luck replaces a gallows,

Luck becomes a murderous weapon,

Beauteous, blooming, bloody mallows

That's the player's paradise

Berserk

Driven by the demons of my past

I roam all over the country

Faithful friends lost blood

I have the last one at hand

He is neither man nor devil

A lump of iron

More human than a thing

More devilish than a murder instrument

The white sinner with angelic hair

A seducer, a traitor

I am now aware of its nature

What remains for me now is to struggle

To walk the dark descent

Keeping an eye on the past

The other on the vengeance that lies

before me

King of the Damned

Once I was a hawk

My ambitions were as high as heaven

And they should lead me to abyssal

depths

So I returned as a falcon of light

More beautiful than an angel

The heart blacker than the night

And yet not entirely dark

I lead the masses cunning and cautious

And many have already left their blood

Cobblestones on the way to power

And yet the blood toll is not paid

My first love will be my last sacrifice

Come join me

My brother,

My sister,

Do you walk the path of raw destruction

with me?

My brother,

Will you squirm and scream

Of your own free will,

A heart full of volition,

For your freedom?

My sister,

Will you break and ignite them,

With burning hatred,

With savage bloodlust,

For our vengeance?

Open, so we can merge

Like steel in the forge,

A will, a sword,

Our shield of brotherhood,

Our blade of sisterhood

Just kidding.

Berserker Armor

- Kentarō Miura -

Trivial meltdown

What they say

They say we have to act accordingly

They say we have to act selflessly

They say we have to act fairly

They say we have to act moderately

They say we have to be civilized

They say we need to be caring

They say we have to be grateful

They say we have to be mindful

They say we have to think logically

They say we have to think in many ways

They say we have to think consistently

They say we have to think differentiated

They say we have to love the culture

They say we have to love people

They say we have to love nature

They say we have to love animals

What I say

I say we can act unconventionally

I say we can act selfishly

I say we can be biased

I say we can act decadently

I say we can be unsavory

I say we can be spiteful

I say we can be ungrateful

I say we can be careless

I say we can think irrationally

I say we can think one-sided

I say we can think ambivalently

I say we can think simple

I say we can judge culture

I say we can disapprove people

I say we can condemn nature

I say we can enslave the animals

And they don't say anything

No Brainer

Oh, my idiot

He is laid-back and carefree

A forgotten empty head

When he feels so happy

Oh, my idiot

He is dull and bubbly.

What a relief to be brain amputated

When he screams „I feel happy!"

When he screams, I feel happy

Then I scream

Heartbreaking g*ng b*ng

A bloody b*tch suffocates

by the filthy bridge

Sweaty wet carwash

Surprisingly slow sl*t rub

Bl*wj*b for money

X-Massacre

Childish cheesy Christmas cheers

Of greenness, unstoppable

Santa's silly season suddenly seems

serious

Santa's end, ending in a

Dark disgusting deadly drama

Of truth, suffocated in

Accidental adult authority analysis

Sturdy Business

My influence on y'all is legendary

Don't make onus my load to carry,

My image is one of a lost generation

I share, I connect, also split a nation

Love your posts

NYs blocks? XoXo

ThX

Just me again on central station,

My eXcuses, changes, new creation

New hair, new friends,

Don't you dare disrupting my self

incination

Hate your posts

Dat botoX? Yea no

You're jealous? You're restentful?

A ridiculous try …

Shamefully it makes me cry

My scandalous tear,

Will make my fans contentful,

See, there's no fall I need to fear.

Digital wholeness

A duality merges

under the unit

Pietro ja Mario Krohnin

- Albert Edelfelt -